# Piano
## Grade Two

A Whiter Shade Of Pale     4

A Winter's Tale     24

Bright Eyes     18

Country Gardens     32

Habañera (from Carmen)     14

Heal The World     28

Holding Back The Years     30

A Musical Joke     8

I Love Paris     16

Les Bicyclettes de Belsize     20

'S Wonderful     10

The Skye Boat Song     6

The Swan (from 'Carnival Of The Animals')     22

To Go Beyond     26

The White Cliffs Of Dover     3

Winter Wonderland     12

© International Music Publications Ltd

First published in 1998 by International Music Publications Ltd

International Music Publications Ltd is a Faber Music company

Bloomsbury House 74–77 Great Russell Street London WC1B 3DA

Series Editor: Mark Mumford

Cover designed by Lydia Merrills-Ashcroft

Music arranged and processed by Barnes Music Engraving Ltd

Printed in England by Caligraving Ltd

All rights reserved

ISBN10: 0-571-53048-6

EAN13: 978-0-571-53048-9

To buy Faber Music publications or to find out about the full range of titles available,
please contact your local music retailer or Faber Music sales enquiries:

Faber Music Ltd, Burnt Mill, Elizabeth Way, Harlow, CM20 2HX England
Tel: +44(0)1279 82 89 82   Fax: +44(0)1279 82 89 83
sales@fabermusic.com   fabermusic.com

# Introduction

In this *More What Else Can I Play?* collection you'll find sixteen popular tunes that are both challenging and entertaining.

The pieces have been carefully selected and arranged to create ideal supplementary material for young pianists who are either working towards or have recently taken a Grade Two piano examination.

As the student progresses through the volume, technical demands increase and new concepts are introduced which reflect the requirements of the major examination boards. Each piece has suggestions and guidelines on fingering, dynamics and tempo, together with technical tips and performance notes.

Pupils will experience a wide variety of music, ranging from folk and classical through to showtunes and popular songs, leading to a greater awareness of musical styles.

Whether it's for light relief from examination preparation, or to reinforce the understanding of new concepts, this collection will interest and encourage all young piano players.

# The white cliffs of Dover

*Words by Nat Burton, Music by Walter Kent*

A song of hope, from the days of World War II. The words speak of 'peace when the world is free.' Singer Vera Lynn, the forces' sweetheart, will always be associated with the tune, but as with all the well-loved and stirring anthems from that time, just about everyone sang along.

This fairly simple, very famous melody has some quite high leaps. It soars upwards like the birds of the song, flying above the clifftops. The left hand part involves some two-part writing, at bars 7 and 15. Think about where the lines are leading and make sure each note sounds with a sense of purpose and belongs where you play it.

# A whiter shade of pale

*Words and Music by Keith Reid and Gary Brooker*

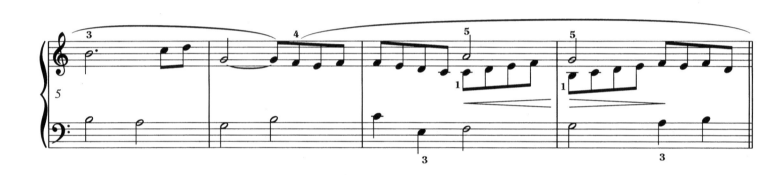

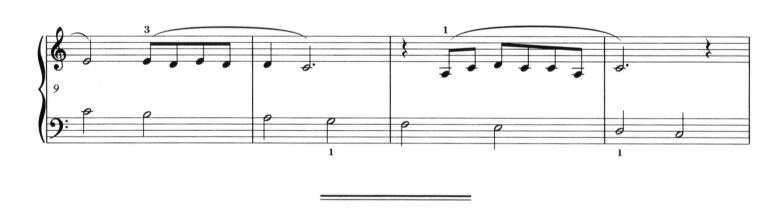

This was the first collaboration of the group Procol Harlem, and the one for which they are mostly remembered. Loosely drawn from J. S. Bach's *Air On A G String*, the song was a number one hit in the UK in 1967. Other recordings include those by the London Symphony Orchestra, the Everly Brothers and Willie Nelson.

Your playing should be very steady and smooth so that the piece has the sense of an elegant procession descending a grand staircase. The left hand takes measured steps down the scale and, even at bars 7 and 8, this idea continues, taken up for just a moment in the upper part in the right hand.

# The Skye boat song

*Traditional*

This song tells the story of Bonnie Prince Charlie's escape from the Scottish mainland to the Island of Skye during the middle of the eighteenth century. This was the end of his hopes to secure the British throne. The song reached the UK top ten in 1986 with a recording by Roger Whittaker and Des O'Connor.

This beautiful folk melody is really quite simple but full of feeling. It uses the same basic rhythmic figure throughout – try to make sure your dotted rhythm sounds smooth rather than jagged. The tune rises and falls in a very balanced way, in four bar statements. Even quite gentle changes in dynamic and tempo, where marked, will be very effective.

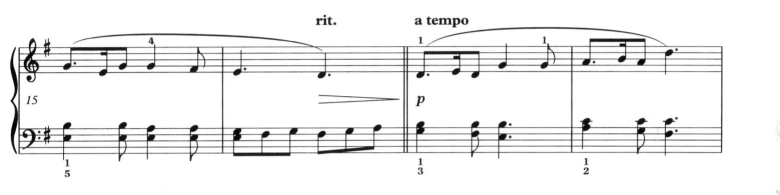

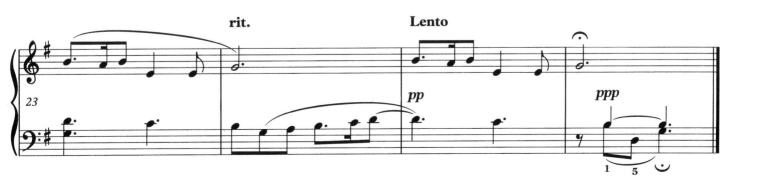

# A musical joke

*Wolfgang Amadeus Mozart*

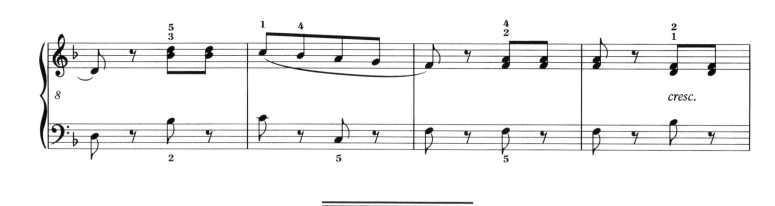

This theme is taken from *Ein Musikalischer Spass* by Wolfgang Amadeus Mozart (1756–1791), a piece that was written literally as a joke. Composed in 1787, the four movement work for two horns and strings was meant as a send up of those composers that Mozart considered to be 'incompetent'. You may also recognise the tune as the theme to the BBC's *Horse of the Year* programme.

The performance direction Scherzando means 'jokingly'. Originally this tune was intended by Mozart to be a playful dig at the popular music of his time. Once you have learned where your fingers should be you can enjoy bringing the piece up to speed and establish a count of one minim to the bar. Give the notes a light, detached feel and take your piano out for a brisk trot!

# 'S wonderful

*Music and Lyrics by George Gershwin and Ira Gershwin*

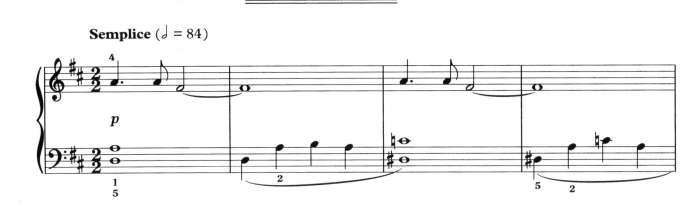

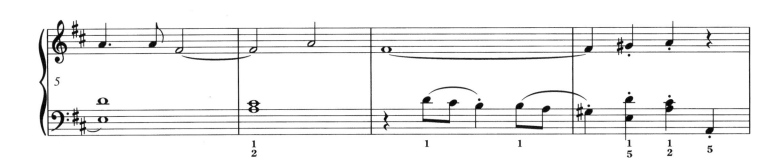

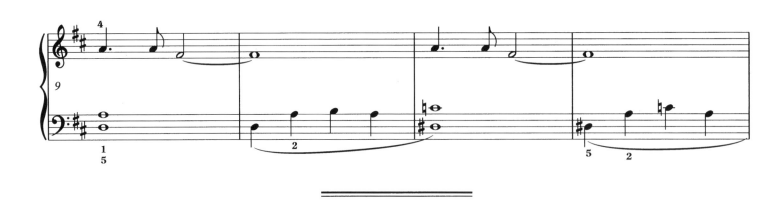

This romantic ballard first appeared in the musical film *Funny Face* (1927). It was also included in no fewer than five other musicals in later years, perhaps the most famous version being Gene Kelly's in the film *An American In Paris* (1951).

The hands tend to take it in turns to move in this piece, the left hand playing a counter melody, but don't be caught off guard, at bar 8, when suddenly both hands are required to move together. There's a change at bar 17, where the lower part moves up into the treble clef. You might find it easier to play these chords if you reach in with your left hand, towards the keyboard.

# Winter wonderland

*Words by Dick Smith, Music by Felix Bernard*

This festive favourite, written in the 1930s, has attracted many recording artists over the years including Elvis Presley, Dolly Parton, The Eurythmics, Bing Crosby and Henry Mancini.

This tune should have a jolly, skipping rhythm. Don't be too strict or rigid about your dotted rhythms here, you can afford to relax just a little, so that they 'swing' easily. The melody should have a sustained, singing quality, while the accompaniment, in the left hand 'trit-trot's underneath, in a more detached style. Don't get muddled up between first and second time bars and listen out for a slight change of mood in the middle section, starting at bar 10.

Francis Day & Hunter Ltd, London WC2H 0EA and Redwood Music Ltd, London NW1 8BD

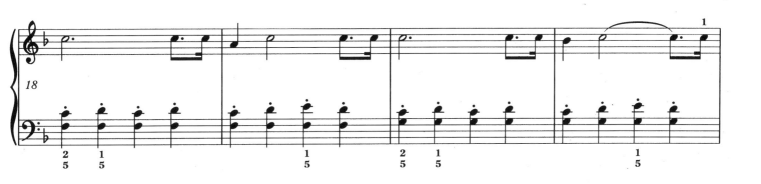

# Habañera
## (from Carmen)

*Georges Bizet*

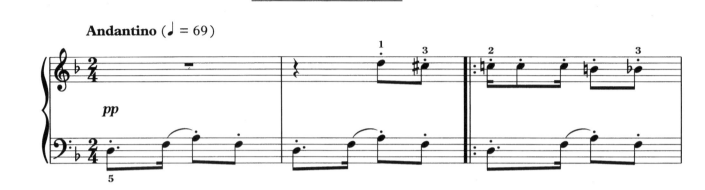

Habañera is taken from *Carmen*, an opera in four acts by Bizet (1838–1875). The opera is set in Spain in the early part of the ninteenth century and depicts Spanish gypsy and peasant life. The first performance of the opera in March 1875 was not particularly well received – by the last act the audiorium was almost empty!

This is a Spanish dance with a very crisp rhythm, imagine castanets! Look carefully at the rhythm of each part and practise hands separately. It's a great one for dynamic control because it calls for quiet attack. There's a sense of things being held under pressure, waiting to explode. Don't miss the fortissimo when it comes!

# I love Paris

*Words and Music by Cole Porter*

This song is taken from the musical *Can-Can* (1953) by Cole Porter (1891–1964), which was later made into a film in 1960 starring Frank Sinatra and Shirley Maclaine. This was the penultimate in the string of musicals from one of America's most prolific popular song writers.

Be sure you are comfortable with the syncopated rhythm in the left hand part. It has a sense of movement but must remain stable to allow the right hand melody to sweep over the top in long phrases. Notice how the tune starts in a minor key and then moves into the major – it feels like the sun has come out!

# Bright eyes

*Words and Music by Mike Batt*

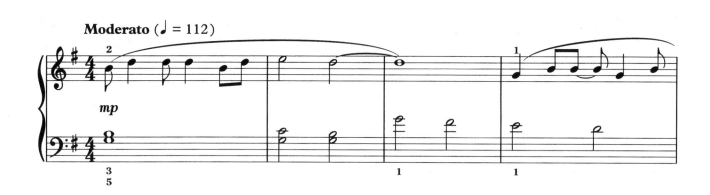

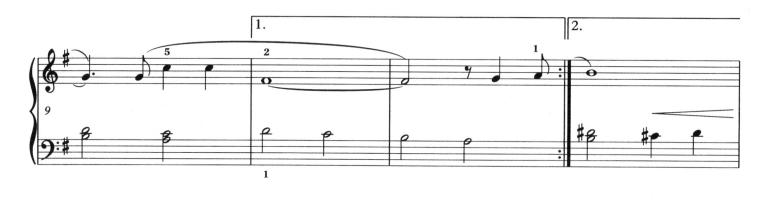

This was the theme song from the animated film *Watership Down*, sung by Art Garfunkel. Although it became the biggest selling hit of 1979, Garfunkel originally had no intention of recording it as a single until American record executives in the UK showed him photographs of fans queuing to see the film. The film itself focuses on the lives of a brave band of rabbits as they search for a peaceful new home.

You need to be alert and keep your eyes peeled here! Take a careful look at the ledger lines which the left hand reaches, you may need to work on recognising notes beyond the stave. Also watch out for first and second time bars and a slight 'change of step' in the phrase starting at bar 13, just running up to the chorus of the song.

# Les bicyclettes de Belsize

*Words and Music by Les Reed and Barry Mason*

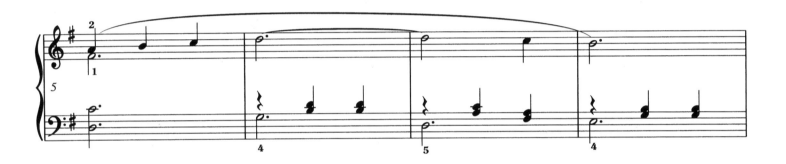

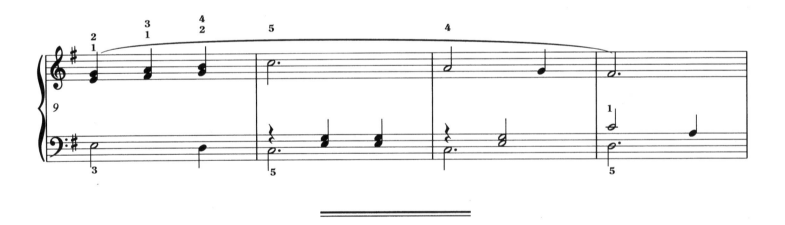

This song was a hit in 1968 for singer Englebert Humperdinck. He had previously performed under the less eccentric title of Gerry Dorsey, but found greater success when re-launched with a name borrowed from the opera composer. The team that wrote this song also wrote the number one hit 'The Last Waltz' and provided Tom Jones with the dramatic 'Delilah'.

This tune is a waltz – three beats in a bar and a slight emphasis on the first beat. The left hand provides a comfortable pulse while the melody flows smoothly above. This requires extra care when there are chords in the right hand. They should enrich the sound without disturbing the melodic line.

# *The swan*
## *(from 'Carnival of the animals')*

*Camille Saint-Saëns*

This piece is taken from the *Carnival Of The Animals*, a musical suite by Camille Saint-Saëns (1835–1921), originally written for two pianos, string quintet, flute, clarinet and xylophone. The Swan was depicted by the cello in the original score. Composed in 1886, the work wasn't published untill 1922 – after the composer's death.

This very romantic tune was written originally to be played by the 'cello. Bring the melody out, as if singing, while the left hand provides a gentle rippling effect in accompaniment. Notice that the left hand begins in the treble clef and then moves between bass and treble as the piece develops. Pay careful attention to the dynamics, especially where a crescendo coincides with a rising scale in the melody.

# A winter's tale

*Words by Mike Batt and Tim Rice, Music by Mike Batt*

**Moderato** (♩ = 108)

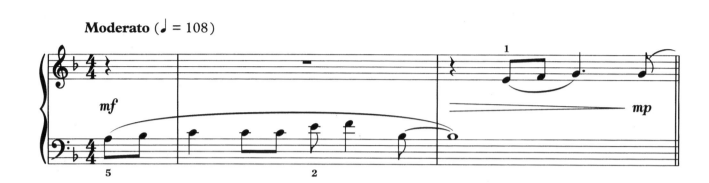

This song, written by Mike Batt and Tim Rice, was recorded by David Essex and became a Christmas hit in 1982, reaching number two in the UK charts. Essex got his first big break when he landed the lead part of Jesus in the rock musical *Godspell* in 1971.

There is quite a lot of variety here. The parts move independently, sometimes bringing counter melodies, which can make it difficult rhythmically. Look for the patterns and phrases and see how they fit together. Try to achieve a sense of calm, forward movement, as of a story unfolding.

# To go beyond

*Words and Music by Enya, Nicky Ryan and Roma Ryan*

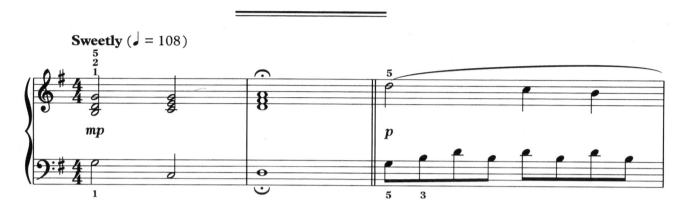

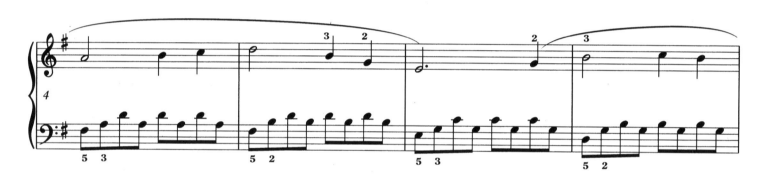

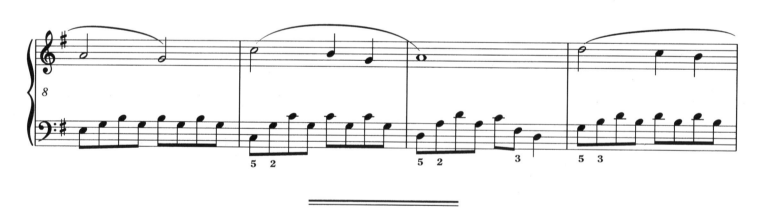

This was one of Irish singer and songwriter Enya's early collaborations with producer Nicky Ryan and lyricist Roma Ryan. Prior to this, Enya sang with her elder brothers and sisters in the group Clannad.

This is a rather dreamy, floating piece which may make a better effect if you apply just a little sustaining pedal. The left hand plays 'broken' chords in a steady, rolling figure. Be sure not to settle in so well that you miss a chord change and avoid allowing the sound of a previous chord to hang over. Perhaps the one surprise is the sense of an 'extra' two beats in the phrase which includes bar 14.

# Heal the World

*Words and Music by Michael Jackson, Prelude by Marty Paich*

Michael Jackson started off as an eleven year old lead singer of the Jackson Five, a group made up of him and his brothers. After leaving the group, he recorded his first solo album *Off The Wall* which remained in the UK album charts for one hundred and seventy-eight weeks. 'Heal The World' is taken from the album *Dangerous* which made it to number one in 1991.

This tune should have a calm and hopeful feeling about it, something you don't want to upset with panicky sounding semiquavers! Look ahead to where the semiquavers come and make sure you can play them smoothly. Also practise the right hand phrases, starting at bar 8, which have a syncopated 'jumping over the beat' rhythm.

# Holding back the years

*Words by Mick Hucknall, Music by Mick Hucknall and Neil Moss*

Simply Red and lead singer Mick Hucknall shot to international stardom with the release of this ballad. It reached number two in the UK charts and number one in the United States. It is featured on the group's debut album *Picture Book*.

This is a piece which does not contain a lot of harmonic movement and is really more about building and sustaining a mood; in jazz and rock terminology a rhythm section might think of it as establishing a 'groove'. Where the right hand plays in thirds try to bring out the upper line, especially in the song's refrain, which starts at bar 19.

# Country gardens

*Traditional*

Thought to date from the 1720s, this pastoral melody was adapted by the composer Percy Grainger in one of the short orchestral works he called 'Fripperies'. Grainger was an active member of the Bristol Folk Song Society and in the early 1900s collected over five hundred folk-songs using a wax-cylinder phonograph.

Your playing should be very bright and breezy here (just typical of an English country garden!). Use a light staccato feel in the left hand and make sure your melodic phrases in the right hand are crisp and rhythmically accurate. Looking ahead and being prepared for changes of hand position will help you achieve this. Try to be clear about the purpose of each dot, don't muddle a staccato dot with a time value dot!